D1297297

THE GOLDFINCHES OF BAGHDAD

The

GOLDFINCHES
OF BAGHDAD

'

Robert

ADAMSON

'

Flood Editions, Chicago

For permission, required to reprint or
broadcast more than several lines, write to:
Flood Editions, P.O. Box 3865
Chicago, Illinois 60654-0865
www.floodeditions.com

ISBN 0-9746902-8-7

Designed by Quemadura

Cover illustration: Garry Shead,
The Arabian Tree (2004)
from *The Ern Malley Suite*.
Courtesy of the artist.

Printed on acid-free, recycled paper
in the United States of America

This publication has been assisted by the
Australian government through the Australia
Council, its arts funding and advisory body.

FIRST EDITION

Contents

PART TWO

for Juno

Part

ONE

A BEND IN THE EUPHRATES

In a dream on a sheet of paper I saw
a pencil drawing of lovers: they seemed perfect,
Adam and Eve possibly. Stepping into reality,
I read lines of a poem on a piece
of crumpled rag I kept trying to smooth—Egyptian
linen, so fine it puzzled to imagine such a delicate
loom. In a flash I saw two dirty-breasted ibis
and heard their heads swish: black bills
swiped the cloudy stream, and in the rushes
I heard needles stitching, weaving features
into the landscape, clacking as they shaped
an orange tree, then switched a beat to invent
blue-black feathers for crows, the pointed
wedges of their beaks. A fox rustles
through wild lantana as I step through into
the garden and, becoming part of the weave,
notice the tide turn, its weight eroding mudbanks,
bringing filth in from the ocean. A raft of flotsam
breaks away, a duckling perched on the thicket
of its hump. I use the murky river for my ink,
draw bearings on the piece of cloth, sketch

3

a pair of cattle egrets bullying teal into flight.
The map's folded away. I travel by heart now,
old lessons are useless. I shelter from bad weather
in the oyster farmer's shack. The moon falls in a
column of light, igniting a glowing epicycle
—this pale spot on my writing table,
these fragments of regret.

A VISITATION

All night, wildfire burned in the tree-tops on the other side of the river. Now it's morning. Smoking embers from the angophoras are landing on the near shore as a yellow-footed rock wallaby limps, dazed, from the scrub, its fur matted, its tail barely able to support its weight. Although wounded, it seems miraculous: the soft yellow of its feet, the hard, sharp black of its claws. It's the first yellow-footer I've seen for more than forty years. It takes me back immediately to a time when I was a kid, rowing my grandfather's tallow-wood skiff across Big Bay: I spotted a mob of four rock wallabies that stood there as I sat silently in the boat and let the tide carry me right by them. One, I noticed, seemed to have mange—it had mottled fur on its back—like the river foxes in those days. Then a panic ran through them: the largest buck bounded, almost flew, straight up an enormous rock; the sheer wildness and ferocity of it shocked me. Afterwards, the atmosphere was thick with an odour unlike anything I recognized. This morning, it's in the air again. I turn to take another look, but the rock wallaby's gone.

THE GREENSHANK

Miklós Radnóti, marched from forced labour
in Yugoslavia back into Hungary, came to rest
near a bend in the Radca, at what his translator
describes as "a strange lonely place" where

the tributary joins "the great river," a marshland
watched over by willows and "high circling birds."
Condors perhaps—they appear in the notes and
poems he was writing—under a foamy sky.

Huddled in a trench with the body of a friend
who'd been shot in the neck, he wrote with a pencil
stub in his notebook: *patience flowers into death.*
His wife's face bloomed in his head.

Thinking of the petals of crushed flowers
floating in a wake of perfume, he wrote to caress her
neck. The fascists' bullets wiped out his patience.
His written petals survive.

Today, we listen to the news of war
here in a river sanctuary my wife's unbending
will has created—horizontal slats of cedar, verticals
of glass—a Mondrian chapel of light.

This afternoon just before dark the first
greenshank arrived from the Hebrides.
Ignorant of human borders, its migration
technology is simple: feathers

and fish-fuel, cryptic colour and homing
instinct. This elegant wader landed on a mooring,
got ruffled in the westerly, then took off again,
an acrobatic twister, and levelled down

onto a mudflat—a lone figure that dashed across
the shore, stood on one leg, then, conducting
its song with its bill, came forward
in a high-stepping dance.

WHISTLING KITES

for Merrill Gilfillan

I anchored out from Sanatorium Rock.
A pair of whistling kites were singing as they circled
their nest in a redgum. My boat settled into the tide
as your book became a map to the exact location of
ancient caves I'd often guessed at, and within, etched
in my mind, rock carvings of mulloway alive with time.

When I opened *Undanceable* and read
your lines on predators who can't hold a tune—
    songless hawks—
the kites' whistling filled the sky above the river.
These raptors a world away from the Solomon
whistle sweet tunes into the face of death; singing
through a sunshower, they drenched me in atonal music.

My lines sang too, slanting into the tide,
their live bait strumming, nylon strings sounding
and your river, the Yampa, flowing out of Dead Horse Bay.
The crows on the shore were American. The songs

8

traced on map and stone swapped places in the air as
    hawks sang.
It was a joy to me, a singing predator

practising ritual—the key to your clear song.
I looked twice at my marks. My river was strange:
the boat was drifting, the anchor ploughing mud, dragging
prehistoric remains—giant feathered salamanders,
flightless ducks—and human singers who carved the
    mulloway
singing from the rock.

EASTER FISH

Tonight in the bright void of our kitchen, my wife
and her mother cooked dinner and talked of brutal places
at the end of the world and meals scraped together

from remnants: thin brown potato skins, tart green
bean soup. We discussed the rituals of Passover.
Charcoal lines from a recent bushfire cross-hatched

the trunks of ghost gums. Outside our kitchen windows,
a butcher bird appeared on the verandah, strutting
the rail and capriciously fluting.

Later our conversation filled an elegant apartment
in Budapest with music. We spoke—carefully, tenderly
perhaps—of the river, the unbroken Danube.

Our minds can flower suddenly sometimes
with monstrous kelp waving in the tide
flowing from old wounds:

brace yourself, cities of the world, against flood,
famine, invasion. Ruin. Now the river's surface
is stretched tight, marbled by a sun setting

in heads indwelling in silence. Puncturing the sky
upstream, a pair of sea-eagles spiral down to their nest.
We steamed our Good Friday fish,

seasoned with sweet basil and the juice of lemons,
and deliciously the taste brought back memories of its
capture: the mauve and silver flanks fading

into a quick death, the small cold flames of phosphorous
lapping our boat's invisible Plimsoll line, the rising
and falling of our breath.

THE VOYAGE

We looked up at Scorpio's tail of stars
curved across light years of night.
We anchored and made love in the dark,

embraced in the cold before dawn and spoke
of Novalis who praised nocturnal light.
Although my thoughts were dark,

you spoke of those who spoke of light
as they moved through the night:
old saints and fishermen following stars.

The river flowed towards morning
until Scorpio grew pale, fading with dawn,
and darkness sailed into light.

WALKING BY THE RIVER

He walked waist-deep
through his thoughts,
emotions, a tangle of vines
and tree-creepers.

His words were finches,
flying before him
as he swung his arms—
scrambled paragraphs.

A waterfall sounded
ahead of his walk,
chipped words cracked
with each step. He came to

a calm place, opulent phrases
in bloom: purple-fruited
pigface, the blackthorn's
blue-black sloe.

EURYDICE AND THE MUDLARK

Sunlight fades the coloured spine
of *What Bird Is That?* The shadow

of your hand marks my face:
wings and the tips of fingers,

coiled hands in the tiny egg
or sac of living tissue,

dredge up a likeness beyond
appearance. Morning unfurls,

I wake and shave. In the mirror
the reflection of a mudlark's tail-fan

echoes the silence of glass.
We hover all day on the surface

of the stream, above a soft bottom,
until moonlight falls again

onto stark white bed-sheets.
The shadow your hand casts

resembles the mudlark, opening
its wings, calling and rocking,

perched in the pages
of my book.

THE FLOATING HEAD

I turned off electricity, pulled telephone cords
out of the wall, saw stars in glass through cedar slats.
I wrapped a scarf around my headache
and looked inside—

an ebbing memory leaving with the tide.
My boat's motor roared and I hurtled across
the river into blazing cold night
then circled back.

Crouched in a corner of the house,
my cat borrows my voice—I talk
to him through the night. The heater
clicks, its pilot light blinks. I scribble

a few lines, pass my fishing rod off
as a lyre. Who needs this bitter tune?
Its distorted chords lull me into numbness.
I bend it over double and pluck.

EURYDICE AGAPE

A preacher came to Calabash Creek
in an expensive four-wheel drive.
He set up in the little park
with his team of technicians.
Bose speakers hung from the gum trees.
The kookaburras started laughing
just before dark.

An oyster farmer's punt, full of
drunks from the Workers Club,
took off from the mudflats and roared
into the night. They called us a bunch
of cunts. Before long the children
from the point were speaking
in tongues. The singing

was fabulous—a woman sang
the Statesboro Blues—and there
was talk of miracles. Then the

preacher spoke of Hell. Suddenly
my arms were full, you started
sobbing, my face was wet with tears.
You were back in paradise.

THE SERPENT

Twenty crows gathered on a branch,
bare in the early summer's heat.
We strung a bow from the willow tree

and used bamboo for arrows.
The afternoon thrummed with locusts.
Clouds at the end of the sky

were alive with thunder that shook
the corrugated iron. We were wet
with sweat—it was a hundred degrees

that day. Granny said, *hot as bloody Hades.*
It was Christmas time—the girls
were up for holidays—and we were

playing under the verandah. The sun
spread a golden glow in the calm
before the gathering storm

as the first snake of the season
came slithering out of the fowl yard,
leaving us its red-checked skin.

EURYDICE AND THE TAWNY FROGMOUTH

On the low arch
above our gate,
he looks out
through a fringe
of feathers,
hunting,
then places one
foot on black
cast iron and ruffles
his head. His other
foot is clenched
in the night air,
held out
in an atmosphere
of waiting—then
unclenched.
Those nights
flying with you
weighed no more
or less than
this.

SINGING HIS HEAD OFF

He stumbles on a rocking pontoon
at the end of his long wharf,
tying things down—greasy ropes

loop around pylons, old tyres hang
from boats. He was ferryman
at Kangaroo Point before the bridge

was built and his horse and punt
decommissioned—it's all gone
into myth now. His arms almost float

in the humid air, he's barely there.
He coalesces around the feeling of loss
of his wife in his stomach.

She's been underground for a week.
He invited no one to the funeral
and has given up speaking.

Cockatoos in the tall melaleucas
above the graveyard drop seed husks
and shake their sulfur crests.

Standing now with his back to the storm,
he straightens and begins to sing—
a deep low moan building

to a howl and a high elemental
keening—his song that could once
make rocks weep.

EURYDICE, AFTER A MIDNIGHT STORM

A koel glides from a nest
abandoned by owls.
We wade in a tide
of humidity. Blue
morning-glory vines
grow in thick night,
undergrowth's stranglers.
The storm breaks
and moves out to sea.
I smell you in the calm
air, an edgy presence,
as house lights
blink on one by one
and Easter's garbled noise
is switched off, then walk
to the edge of the river
and listen to the tide
rush downstream.

LETTER TO EURYDICE

Watercolour moon, the window-panes
fogged up. Outside, the river

slips by; an overhanging blackbutt
branch inscribes the surface

with a line across foaming run-off.
Living near mudflats I'm protected

by mangroves: in winter
the southerly rakes their curly heads,

the green skirts are my windbreak.
At the Fork these summer thoughts

are silted up and become obscure:
it's more than halfway into a big ebb

and my mind's a dark moat. If you
get this far—*watch it*—and step

on my dreams, you'll find
they've been pulped. It's only flight

that matters here; take a break and fling
your next thought into the tide.

In these parts, the lyrebird must carry
its own cage on its back

through swamps—I once believed this.
But yesterday the bird suffered a stroke.

"It keeps falling to the ground," the ranger
said, "nothing can be done." It's time

to commiserate with this creature,
all songbird but not quite lyre.

EURYDICE COMBS HER HAIR

We reach the end of a bay
and cut in through mangroves.
Our boat hits the bottom,
kicks up mud and sand.
Crossing a deep hole,
the water changes texture—
the surface becomes choppy—
and the trees along the shore here
are the colour of salmon fillets.
A whipbird cracks its call
down a sandstone escarpment
as we anchor up and the sun
sets behind clouds. I sing to you,
wherever you are. In the dark's
chill I can smell your hair,
even though you're
beyond reach.

EURYDICE ON FIRE

A shapeless field of mist above the river's
surface, drifting. At first light the head

of a tree emerges, then black sticks
from oyster racks. The mist

parts as it rolls across
a channel pole's yellow marker—

another level of watching settles
in thinking the mist

forms ribbons and leaves
wisps of itself

in mangrove branches.
My head starts burning,

jagging its hurt deeply: here's
a woman caught in time,

unable to grow old.
She's never said a word

I've heard of. Can she speak?
Do I have any choice?

I step clear, fully alight,
for long enough to think

What's to say? Her voice
echoes the absence.

Torchlight flares on the book's
cover—reading's difficult in the boat—
and you wonder, is the helmsman
distracted by light?
On this river
there's only one destination, that dock
on the other side. The pages
are smeared by yellow light-beams:
What time of day is it?
What day of the month?
We continued the crossing—flowering gums,
bees flying by polarized light—then watched
a shape forming, an emerald blur of wings
at the periphery of torchlight, a bee-eater
hovering over words, over the hive
of the book.
We taste honey
on our tongues—an orange beak flashes—
and read to one another in pitch dark,
carried on the wings of words.

EURYDICE IN SYDNEY

What was he thinking while I was gone?
Was his mind still doing time in his head,
dancing in abstract darkness?

Pain comes and goes. I notice things
I hadn't before: the city ibis stitching its voice
to the wind between car park and street.

I think of going shopping with him.
Bogong moths in a shaft of sunlight
flutter beneath the blue trees

of a shadowy Hyde Park. Does
Sydney Harbour still exist? Depends
on how his voice murmurs

late into night as he drinks, rustling
still with that old ardour, trailing ribbons
of smoke and blood.

THINKING OF EURYDICE AT MIDNIGHT

My Siamese cat's left a brown
snake, its back broken, on my desk.
The underground throbs outside my window.
The black highway of the river's crinkled by a light
westerly blowing down. I want to give praise
to the coming winter, but problems
of belief flare and buckle under
the lumpy syntax. The unelected
President's on the radio again,
laying waste to the world.

Faith—that old lie. I drag up
impossible meanings and double divisions
of love and betrayal, light and dark.
Where on earth am I after all these years?
A possum eats crusts on the verandah,
standing up on its hind legs.
My weakness can't be measured.
My head contains thousands of images—
slimy mackerel splashing about in the murk.

My failures slip through fingers pointed
at the best night of my life. This one.

The cold mist falls, my head floats in a stream
of thinking. Eurydice. Did I fumble? Maybe
I was meant to be the moon's reflection
and sing darkness like the nightjar. Why
wouldn't I infest this place, where the
sun shines on settlers and their heirs
and these heirlooms I weave
from their blond silk?

Part

TWO

YELLOW BITTERN

At Ulladulla
a bittern puffs out its neck feathers,
head between wings—

slits of eyes tight in the wind
flinging sand, hammering grains of stone
against it.

Our bird of words falls apart—
its wings without vowels,
its head empty of tough money.

O bittern, come off it, talk to us
about when we were young: that first
kiss hissing as she bit my tongue.

GANG-GANG COCKATOOS

In the outer suburbs we pass under them,
dark grey with white stripes, in swishing
fractals of tropical vegetation,
screeching metal songs,

swinging upside down, juggling
pine-nuts—very funny but beyond us.
My state of mind's stencilled on the
footpath, my footprints identical

to gang-gangs': there's a crevice in my
forehead, with a slash of grey, but overall my
head's a red hood. As for my tremulous
tone of voice, who'd believe such

flickering convictions? I smile because
things are so pleasant here: my lightweight
cotton top's cool on humid days, and the
southerly each afternoon

ruffles my feathers, so that sometimes
I chuckle. Since my children left New
York and set up house in exclusive
suburbs—well? The colossal

phone bills, the visits maybe once
in three years, snaps of the kids dressed
as gang-gang chicks in a delightful garden,
the daughter-in-law pecking for money,

private schools to teach them "Hello Cocky"
—it's "swell." I've never used that word,
just wanted to indicate I'm familiar
with the tone used in the cages

of middle America. Gang-gang women
know the score and take it on the chin:
we scorn the first person singular because
at night we drift beyond it.

ECLECTUS PARROT

Bright green, scarlet-bellied, black-billed bird
crash lands in campsite. Fire burns cub's fingers.
The scoutmaster flicks the billy with a switch
and growls. Smoke billows and turns brown.

This picture-on-a-biscuit-tin is being
painted as we read: the politician as artist
on his weekend fishing trip. His son,
an eagle scout, hammers the billy

with a triangle. Now hundreds
of budgerigars wheel across a low sky:
the whole jumble's put together from used
landscapes garnished with raptors.

The Minister for Defence has news for these
creatures. He mimics the eclectus parrot—
his face turns red like its satin belly—but *his*
black beak's genetically engineered for speech.

MAJOR MITCHELL'S PINK COCKATOO

In the Mallee, dodging crooked branches of mulga
trees, she waits like a sundial for our caravan,
her clear voice a distinct falsetto attracting
passion police and painted quail. Time the cracker
keeps her harmful—her sweat's a fixative, printing alluring
shadows on skin, sketches intricate with pain. We track her
by the dark tan wickerwork winds make of her nests.
The world crumbles into red sand as she takes
my place—neither bird nor feathered tease
of her flock—and I walk out, prepared to let fall—
look—my frame, tail-shaped, fanning air.
Getting nowhere.

RED-NECKED AVOCET

Wading in a lake, its entrance
to the sea blocked, our legs
illuminated by white-hot
mantles burning kerosene
in pressure lamps, it was all
detail. Could we know
the avocets were victims?
The acid from our joint
imagination billowed
behind us, a killing wake:
we were all eyes. Huge prawns
kicked up under our toes,
then zapped away into weeds;
the wings of black swans fanned
our desire to eat the avocet's
fragile, mottled eggs. We tried
to feed one of the chicks
boiled prawns; she looked
angelic as she shuddered.
The fire on the sand crackled
with dead bulrush canes and spat

whizzing, popcorn-sized embers;
flames licked the black
of the moon. Our cotton clothes
soaked up the smoke's breath.
We were drunk with salt
and sand, with killing, eating
prawns, talking rubbish, having
fun. Avocets migrated from our
thoughts into words and went
skidding into sound as they
too became human.

THE RUFF

It's difficult to describe the ruff.
This bird's a live metaphor, puffing
its plumage into simile. A rough
attempt at meaning: though a
waterbird, it dances onshore.

Its colours? Sepia, cream, and
specks of red. These tones bleed well
for watercolourists, but a cock ruff
in display looks top-heavy, often
toppling over into absurdity or worse.

Ruff's a word from the sixteenth century:
feathers goffered into ornaments
for sex. Ritual is human. These cock
birds blow up by instinct, strutting
as if to get across how inhuman

they are, how utterly bird. They
dance in lines of ruff music; some
have suggested that a feather's cadence,
once heard, conducts this dance—
a puffed pose, its head hidden by dark

cowling and the eyes blinded by display.
The ruff's ways delight us if we have
a sense of humour or a dash of
madness: the way of the ruff
is for folk who take themselves

seriously, for this bird's habits
contradict words, art, and human
silence. A ruff occurs at the fringes
of things, in the gap between it
and words. Ruff.

RAINBOW BEE-EATERS

Wings fuelled
by the knowledge of bees

turning on axles of air
each crescent beak

an orange-coloured talisman
Once snowy-headed elders

gathered honey bags
in turpentine forests

feathery blurs eating bees
hovering miracles

alongside ancient cliffs
flashed brightly

Your film exposed to them
transparencies

to stay love by catching day
light on pages

the translucent calligraphy
of wings

THE RAVENS: AFTER TRAKL

The ravens launch themselves
into the air

dropping harsh calls as they
sail across midday;

their shadows follow them
along the glassy river—

you can see them at times
almost resting.

They rupture the silence
at twilight. At other times

their sound is like the stench
of drunks bickering over

carrion in the beer garden.
Look up into the spotted

gum tree: they fly off
like a funeral procession,

their caws small shudders
of rapture.

THE PEACH-FACED FINCHES OF MADAGASCAR

I cart home sugarbags of coke from the gasworks.
My hands mark the cream-painted icebox. My father
throws spuds on the fire, sending sparks up the flue.

On the hill outside, trucks growl and strip their gears.
I imagine the peach-faced finches of Madagascar.
After tea, Dad slumps in his chair, tall brown bottles

standing empty on the table. At school each day I fail
my tests. My mother's face hardens when I try to speak.
She irons starch into my sister, from her straight black

hair to her school uniform's box pleats. In the back yard,
cuckoo chicks squawk from a magpie's nest. The hedge
man's finished clipping hedges along our street.

My brothers bob down to do their homework, into
the learning stream, heading for their lives,
biting the heads off words.

THE DOLLARBIRD

As the family listened to the reading
of the will, dollarbirds were landing,
summer migrants thudding into soft
magnolia trees in bloom. It seems
I'll be able to free this captive life
of my mind, let it fall from my eyes
like fish scales and just walk away—
now she'll be okay financially at least.
My conscience, the bully, keeps honing
these blunt threats daily. How much
freedom will she take, how many lozenges
of grief in brown paper bags? I'll scatter
rotten fruit on the terrace and every flying
insect on the northern peninsula will loop
and scuttle in droves for the feast. Dollarbirds
will hawk for them in the air. Translucent,
she glides through my thoughts reading
The Divine Comedy in the compartment
I've filed her in. Bad? Sure, but there's more
housework to be done in my head today.
Pawpaws rot efficiently—they attract pests

from miles away, hovering and crawling.
As she listens, her cheeks glow, her thoughts
swerve as elegantly as dollarbirds gathering
the words to strike. There's a cavil, a hiccup
and a shudder down her spine. Thirty years
of gibberish, resentments drenched in perfume,
years of love and an inkling she could be wrong.
Can I siphon off the fertilizing fantasy and let
passion wither like old skin? Unpleasant
metaphors vanish, migrate back to where
those green-feathered beakies come from:
a dollarbird tumbles as it flies above
magnolia trees in bloom.

THE COWBIRD

This is not poetry—this bird's turkey-head
has a craw that produces crap—its chicks,
    feeding, get covered in a stench
    you could compare

to the breath of an alcoholic cane toad
that's feasted on a bucket of rancid pork.
    The descriptive drift
    throws up this internationalist:

the hoatzin (pronounced *what-seen*),
lives on the banks of the Orinoco River
    flowing through the central
    plains of Venezuela.

Young hoatzins dive-bomb the surface
from their nests overhead, swim
    underwater then pull themselves
    back up into the trees

with their clawed wing-tips.
The idea of these creatures has been known
     to drive scientific investigators
     crazy: infesting the imaginations

of phytochemists from within,
they create themselves from the dark
     whims of their hosts, parachuting
     in through their eyes.

Good students have fried their brains
contemplating the mating habits
     of the cowbird—they are, however, pure
     joy to confessional poets,

who weave them in as tropes as they write poems
concerning their wedding night, in which they
     consummate their bliss oozing
     the milk of *what-seens.*

THE GREY WHISTLER

There's a man knocking at the door.
He was a friend once; these days
he's on his last legs—body and soul
stitched together by the court of petty
sessions, he makes a living serving writs.
Samples of deliverance are considered
by the jurists, so I provide details
of my shame—by drawing, for example,
a tropical whistler. Once called the brown
whistler, it lives in mangrove swamps
and their adjoining rainforests. This bird
creates hatches in dense foliage: you can
reach into them and salvage a shabby
pillow of whistler-down created by
tropical humidity, as soft as the texture
of human sorrow. Our friend's ex-wife
was a model who pranced the catwalks
in gowns embroidered with luminous
flecks from the whistler's pinions—
the handiwork of that one-eyed Italian
who made his name in Paris. I have some

fabric in a basket—let's turn it into a hood.
Next time he knocks, I'll pull it over my
head and act dumb. *Peggy, there's a good
girl, stay calm—I'm a husk each time
you wince.* But the knocking at the door
continues. In the backyard lemon tree,
there's a city crow coughing its lungs up.
As the night goes on, the man outside
becomes the Grey Whistler.

THE FLAG-TAILED BIRD OF PARADISE

*(George W. Bush instructed "the enemy" to hold up white
flags and stand twenty metres away from their tanks,
promising that if they did, they would be spared.)*

Thought to be extinct, they are appearing
through the red mist, their white tails
waving at blunt helicopters
splattering the earth. These creatures
from paradise play dead when attacked:
they freeze, clamped to a branch, the tiny
flags of their tails barely shimmering in
broken sunlight. They once lived
in jungles on islands in the Pacific,
but haven't been found dead there
since 1958. Some escaped to Arabia:
sold to collectors and bred in captivity,
they were taken up by zoos, kept in palaces
and inbred. Flunkies fed them and sultans
hovered about them, marvelling at how
they became extraordinary in their
deformities—their cream-coloured plumage

shot through with pale, beautiful rainbows,
their eyes enormous, pink, and their
flag-tails heavy—almost too heavy
to hold up, but not theirs
to withhold.

THE GOLDFINCHES OF BAGHDAD

These finches are kept in gold cages
or boxes covered in wire mesh;
they are used by falcon trainers as lures,
and rich patriarchs choose these living ornaments
to sing to them on their deathbeds. Their song is pure
and melodious. A goldfinch with a slashed throat
was the subject of a masterpiece painted in the
sixteenth century on the back of a highly
polished mother-of-pearl shell—it burns
tonight in Baghdad, along with the living,
caged birds. Flesh and feathers, hands
and wings. Sirens wail, but the tongues
of poets and the beaks of goldfinches burn.
Those who cannot speak burn along with the
articulate—creatures oblivious to prayer burn
along with those who lament to their god.
Falcons on their silver chains, the children
of the falcon trainer, smother in the smoke
of burning feathers and human flesh.
We sing or die, singing death
as our songs feed the flames.

Part
THREE

FISHING IN A LANDSCAPE FOR LOVE

This is swampland, its mountains
worn down by the wings of kingfishers
flying back to their nests. Crows
are black feathers

saving me from morning.
I talk to them as if we're friends,
they look at me sideways.
When I offer them fish they eat it.

Swamp harriers whistle as they do
slow circles through the azure—
let's talk about the azure.
Descriptions of place

can't imitate the legs of prawns
moving gently in the tide
from which the azure takes on meaning.
I put them into a mosquito-wire cage

and lower them from the jetty,
they jump from their sleep
on the dark of the moon.
Bait is all that matters here—

love's worn down into sound
and is contained in what I say,
these dead words feeding on live ones,
these ideas thrown to the crows—

they don't come back.
Love needs live bait,
it doesn't behave
like a scavenger.

BRAHMINY KITE

Humidity envelops my boat, black mould
embellishes its trim. There are mullet-gut stains
on the seats. Tides flood in across the mudflats
and small black crabs play their fiddle-claw
with a feeble left bow, day in, night out.
My hand swoops to catch a lure.
Talons pierce scales and a heart.

We grasp the core only gradually
of each other's compressed midnights—
black roses flowering in sandy-eyed dawns,
memories stowed to starboard, where a
brahminy's wings catch first light.
How did we manage it, sailing
on—weathering

leagues of years? We're a far cry now from
beating wings and arched poetic myths:
the swell's escalator takes us up over the top
of the world into white crests and gull-squawk.
Now there are fields of light to relinquish

and dolphin fish skittering around
markers, slicing apart an oily sea.

Off Barrenjoey, the kite hits thermals,
then lifts into a triple rainbow stained with
yellowtail blood and slime. Its beaked head fits over
my face, sea-spray stings my eyes. In the haze
beyond tiredness, its wings cut through
an atmosphere thick with salt
and the glint of fish scales.

THE FIRST CHANCE WAS THE LAST

Down sandstone steps to the jetty—always
the same water, lights scattered across tide.
Remember, we say, the first time.
Our eyes locked into endless permission,

this dark gift. Why can't I let go
and be the man in your life—not the one who writes
your name on the dedication page; whatever
the name, you know who I write for,

you know how private, how utterly selfish
these musings are. This is your image,
crafted in the long hours away. The house
rocks, money comes and goes, fish

jump against tide. The children grow
and go out into the world. The bleak eye
turns, my tongue speaks with ease—a rudder
steering the stream of words into their

daily meanings. I cried out when you weren't
here, I smashed my fist against stone. Art was stone.
A red glow cracked the kitchen window. I carved
the roast and served it to our cats.

Signposts point the way. Bitter laughter stings,
my black heart beats. This way to the shops
and gallery in ordinary day. Clap your
hands against my ears, turn off the lights—

you stay. Is it *always* you? Shapes change,
music becomes a pool of melancholy seawater
distilled in sun, slapping rock, then a seagull's eye
reflecting a shoal of whitebait alive with death.

Love makes an art that walks in a son
and moves a daughter. We move
through time and sing in the light:
the first chance was the last.

POWDER HULK BAY

for John Firth-Smith

Blocks of sandstone suspended in air
above the roadway on Old Spit Bridge.
Hours painted black. Black-capped
terns catching chips in the park.

We talked for twenty summers thinking it
meant something: sand sticking to sweaty limbs,
rasping voices buffeting families on the beach,
children, streaks of cloud moving through

afternoon light. Sails flaring on the blue surface
of the bay—slabs of meaning. Each painting
holds one: friends gone, scratches of writing
remembering what we *should* have said.

A peppercorn tree by the harbour shakes with cicadas
making their throbbing note stick. One day a great bull
shark swam up to the side of our boat, almost touching.
Sealice scabbed its gills, trailing a shredded wire trace

from a fishing line. It kept shaking its head, rolling
an eye as if to take us in. We froze, held the oars tight
and still. Whatever we said rose up into the currawong's
melodic fluting. A wing's streak of white

is all that separates us from the dead. Encased
in a wave of cicada sound, we're a hair's breadth
away from live bait—and water the colour
of paradise, an indigo black with news.

WINTER NIGHT

for Kevin Hart

In the darkness beyond our garden fence,
a white-tailed water rat. Our cat crouches
in ambush in the mango tree. Down
below, an amateur fisherman flicks a lure

at racks of oysters near the shore,
then gives up and takes a swig of whisky.
Ah, the way that first drink braces.
A motorboat roars by—no lights—

the black river swallows it, leaving
behind a swirl of fumes. The surface
reflects the glow from our house
and the chuckling call of a nightjar.

Stars fracture the sky with light. The cat
keeps playing with weird marsupials,
the hook wound in my finger stings
like hell. As I come up from the wharf,

a flying fox rattles in the banana palms—
I hear the long whisper of its beating wings
follow me up the stairs. The stars flicker
letters from a dead god's alphabet.

ELEGY FROM BALMORAL BEACH

for Arkie Deya Whiteley

A beach. Small waves and a shark net.
Moonlight on a fig tree, the bay a black mirror.

Music coming from a house, an exquisite guitar.
Tonight, there's nothing more bitter.

Resonating chords float above the school yard,
night birds beat the humid air. The ebb tide

exposes the moon's haul: squabbling seagulls
slicing open the body of a drowned rat.

A light flickers, a newspaper floats. Doc Watson's
playing sounds like a waterfall, almost gentle.

Tonight the harbour's incandescent.
You arrive in an empty boat.

MEMORY WALKS

Ideas of memory walks
replace our need for narrative
Our heads flicker projecting their stories

There's a boat at the end of each tale
and the weary can just paddle out
onto the stream

water sparkling with minerals good enough to drink
Each stroke of the oar stains it
with inky clouds of thinking

Here we come across the node
of the fractured sentence that indicates
an overload so we dump our ballast of loves

There's a couple of lives
and the brave among us can choose both
The consequences are there each morning

flaring away in the bathroom mirror
staring over the coffee and toast
the space where lovers come clean

about their strolls
and what they scratched on public walls
the night before

ON NOT SEEING PAUL CÉZANNE

I think of the waste, the long
years of not believing the
tongue pretending

in the midst of words
to speak, to keep walking
that bend in the road

I cursed myself for not having spoken

The blank sheets of air could have added

Words smudged out and revised with a colour

stroked instead of butting
coming to the shape by layers, stumbling
in from the corners and rubbing out the hard light

The countless fish flapping on boards
Have they just disappeared?
there's no way

back to the water to catch
again that possible
colour

Outside the window in the black night
mosquitoes gather under floodlights on the pontoon
until the empty westerly blows

Everything that matters comes together
slowly, the hard way, with the immense and tiny details,
all the infinite touches, put down onto nothing—

each time we touch
it begins again, love quick brush strokes
building up the undergrowth from the air into what holds

ÉVENTAIL: FOR MERY IN PARIS

Writing this in sepia ink on a Japanese fan,
pain slants my calligraphy
this way, sex just under the cap of my skull.

Dreams taunt your existence
as you swish by in raw silk
until the words I use lose meaning

and my best lines sag like limp
old lace. This metaphor thick with blood
trembles as my mind approaches the blank

folds in rice paper, writing
on your arms, this scrawl scrolling
through you, each letter a link in the chain

between my head and the bed, a text
of splintering syllables in which
time comes apart, prickling your skin—

the joke's our meaning, gnarled
with the word-knots coming undone
where your breast shines with sepia

ink and the sheets blot out thinking.
Smudged with love, your bum's a haze
of lavender oil as I rub this in.

ELIZABETH BISHOP IN TASMANIA

The hopscotch map on the pavement
puzzled her at first: a boy mucking
around with a hoop caught her eye
and she put them together

as a sharp new drink. A wizard with flowers,
no good with bereavement,
she continuously topped up her bright stanzas
and tucked her emotions away

in print. The critics write about her
scrupulous control, her management
of traditional forms alongside her *vers libre*—
hardly her style in life itself,

where she found oblivion in tides
of drink. She said she wanted
"closets, closets and more closets!" Once a year,
when a new moon rose in her head, she set

sail for the south—nobody knew where
exactly—her subterfuge being her poetry,
which gave cryptic clues. Secretly,
she was Tasmanian. Bring me

flying fish on a crinkled ocean, seahorse
and Patagonian toothfish—the icy crags
turn pink tonight: there's a kissing of flesh
as the eyes dim and invisible birds sing.

LETTER TO ROBERT CREELEY

I've heard the system's closing down. It's good
reading in books, old friend, your words about
what a friend is, if you have one. These
days I often think of Zukofsky
just throwing in the word
"objectivist" and how it works
as well as any label could. These
days we're just words away
from death and I think
I've finally learnt to listen (your love
songs seem wise now that the years
have steadied my head) as you turn hurt
without sentiment to gain. I thought
of your clear humour when my father
was dying of cancer. I asked about the pain
and he spun me a line: "it feels like a big
mud crab having a go at my spine."

LETTER TO TOM RAWORTH

Before escaping
from the clock
self imposes
on the page
in those days
I could hardly talk
and called you
in my head Tom
Raw Worth

There was some
kind of criminal
in that poem
of yours called
Morrell

The brown endpapers
of *Moving* were doors
I slunk through

I lived in those pages
free from narrative
speaking a language
I could read not utter

The light led me
through chambers
of murmurings
calling me I
thought in the
pitch of your voice
though it was
streets not spires
where the books
were not blocks
of stone or holy
glass but a sly
side of the
mouth code
serious song
that wouldn't
parry or fuck
with you
for exclaiming
these lines are
wonderful these

tough folk are not
embarrassed by
wonder

Morrell's keys
to the prison jingled
as you walked up walls
your head took
the weight and made
the weirdness
surrounding me
release small change
to pay for sheets
of creamy Fabriano
that were soon
transformed into
a kind of folding
money so the
Morrells could
pay for their keys
and on each page
I made appeared
that watermark
Raw Worth

THE FLOWTHROUGH

for the Johns

We loved the front, your wall of words,
and the fact that snatches made sense
to the professors. We read
The Double Dream of Spring
and argued fiercely about whether
it was the way to go—tied knots
in your tangles, tendrils of phrases
that wound their way round our pages.
Those were the days we exist in now—
we hacked through time
and came out twisted. Gaping holes
in space, we fed on sentences stitched
together with a grammar that was streetwise,
though with impeccable manners that always
got us through the gates. The mix of sweetness
and a ferocity that could burn holes
was what I admired most in *Some Trees*—
those poems were places I made friends in.
I remember Tranter standing in a classroom
reading them, his laughter edged with irony

and kindness. Ashbery days, when poets
were drunk on code within code,
when language cracked open and showed us
the power of whimsy and a dark abyss
that said "perhaps" as it echoed.

NOT A PENNY SONNETS

Remember the club sandwich?

GIG RYAN

I

A book launch, plates of water biscuits.
"There's always the club sandwich," you said.
But the corporate types didn't get it—they were
busy being freaks—so we spliced letters into words
as verbal tattoos, using anything we'd written,
digging our biros in. A girl drives by
in a low-slung Torana. Remember the suburbs,
those days of ordinary defeat? Using street directories
so out of date they didn't show the streets?
We had dreams of driving racing cars. These days
we can afford to trade quips at the Intercontinental,
go to funerals, throw out old affections. Drinking
beer and double gins, I'm talking
but nothing seems to grip.

2

I've written my response before you speak:
"Well, fiddle-de-dee," we said to the police,
walking onto the illuminated page,
being freaks, digging our biros in. We honed
our beaks on cuttlefish bones from your baptismal
swim, stringing along the corporate types, filling
shot glasses to the brim in our separate skins.
Cracks? Take a bite and your teeth might ache
with old affections and lost destinations.
We sharpened the edge for decades, drinking hard,
looking for something to blame. Remember smoking
ready-mades? You demanded things—impossible—
from me. I had nothing, not a penny to my name,
just references, chips, and lemonade.

3

We scoff at good luck from the Intercontinental,
flash Medicare cards before signing anything.
Our biros dig into *Gone with the Wind*, breathing
air-conditioned memories in separate skins—
goose pimples, anti-fashion, enemies, and friends.
Back on the street, we take in the city.
A Torana spins its wheels, skeins of brown smoke
clog the pavement—she's gone. But we're still
standing here, talking, destroying words.
The club sandwich? Well, fiddle-de-dee. We believe
nothing: the shredded trust, the corporate types—
just limping figures in dressed skin. The life
we mocked surrounds us—distracted,
but the tide keeps coming in.

THE APOSTLEBIRD

The housed is packed;
He doesn't need to change the act.
JAMES MCAULEY

The Angry Penguins were a self-corrupting
rabble, their madrigals dangerous music.
Come now, it was a lark my dears:
the students called me the Apostlebird
(after my pet) for years. Then
I actually witnessed the beast, a crucifix
in one hand, a jug of afterbirth in the other.
It was song, some jazz, a few black jokes,
the odd perk—nothing sexual—

that snipped away their insolence
and tampered with the masks.
I wanted my quiddity to float through the halls,
bumping up against the ancient forms,
and held to what I knew would hold—
feathers sprouting from the arms of a boy
who played the black swan. The enemy
couldn't write a sentence. Atheists brought on
marsupials, living props to prove

that life was chaos. I might as well have
spoken up for the hazards of sin,
god damn it—the students with distemper,
protesting against a just war. I carried
a wild animal around, hoping it might
attack someone and teach me more
about guilt. When my wife lit the bonfire
on cracker night, its flames exposed my face
against a floozie's thigh—the silk

stockings, the birds of paradise stuffed
and hanging in glass "as if in flight."
The jungle followed me down corridors of power.
Sick bastards, I wanted them to confront
the living beast. I kept its world in my head—
protecting the family, knowing that
even a careless word might start the rot—
but towards the end succumbed and closed the eyes
of that sinister bird.

DAVID ASPDEN'S RED THEME

Parrots have subverted it, the
red-capped lorikeets completely green—
one pulls its talons together
into a little arthritic bunch.

Mondrian painted Hitler's moustache
with red pigment and linseed oil.
Saint Paul must have been considering red
as he dipped his quill in Christ's wounds.

Red spots on a double-bar's head—
an ornithologist plucks
a feather, thereby furthering
a breeding project.

Red on the wattle of a silky cock
waking a small town, where fishermen market
the last of the swordfish. Sunlight on lumpy oceans
where albatross dive for red hooks.

DAVID ASPDEN'S YELLOW TREE

The yellow tree's
a shadow so faint it's invisible

we know it's there
oh we know exactly where

the painting will sail on to meet
its maker's grandchildren

one day in a stainless museum
they'll look up and say

nothing but turn inward
as the tree seems to be asking us to do

so that you may perhaps
meet some traveller there

and walk awhile
some unknown place

talk will smudge the air
and float from your mouths

you will shine
with a light the painter

knew
was there

inside
somewhere

FLANNEL FLOWERS FOR JUNO

We walk along a crumbling bush track,
the full moon dropping through gums,
down through the sparse limbs,
their shredded bark hanging by balance—
thinking in fragments.

The air's damp and sweet.

The sounds of the river are softened
while you carry the rest of the world in your head
and I empty myself of memories one
word at a time.

They sink behind us onto the floor of the bush.

Your face shines with competence,
your hair flows, I hold your warm hand as we walk.
It feels miraculously alive compared to my
dry mouthings.

Whatever we pass by seems very old.
Twigs petrified into black glass crack under our feet.
A tawny frogmouth owl looks at us from a dead branch
unblinking, immobile.

I can't ask you for forgiveness.
Words aren't part of this landscape.
The weight of what I've done grinds away at my knees,
the joints of my bones scrape away the word "jelly."
My head floats on the path beside you, its hair
speckled pollen from flowering gums.

You turn to gaze into a sandstone cave.

Above the entrance, flannel flowers
grow from the roots of an ancient fig,
their blossoms closed against the dark.

REACHING LIGHT

Where was it we left from?
We say the journey's up, but maybe

memory sinks deeper.
Our journey so far

has been quiet, the only
incident being that rock dislodged

as he spun around on his heel.
What was that stuff—brimstone?

The first slice of sunlight glanced off
a slab of dark marble that turned to glow.

His back moved ahead of me—
his curls, shoulders,

that neck. What new bone was he inventing
in his shuffling head, what chance

that a doorway would appear and then a house?
The dark supported me, comfortably

behind me, a cradle woven from
demon hair. As I rose

and climbed toward day, his turning head,
those eyes—strips of memory,

silver tides, moons rising over the
rim of the world—

brought back the day we were married,
standing in fine rain, then escaping from family,

sex by a rolling surf in a high wind, velvet
heavens and the stars omens:

calendars, clocks, zodiacs—
straight, bent signs.

Acknowledgments

Grateful acknowledgment is made to the editors of the following anthologies and journals in which many of these poems first appeared: *The Age, Australian Book Review, The Best Australian Poems 2003, The Best Australian Poetry 2003, The Best Australian Poetry 2004, Boxkite, Heat, Jacket, The Manhattan Review, Meanjin, The Newcastle Poetry Prize Anthology, Poetry International, Poetry Review* (U.K.), *Salt Lick Quarterly, Southerly, Sydney Morning Herald*, and *Verse Daily*.

Earlier versions of some poems were published as "New Poems" in *Mulberry Leaves: Selected Poems 1970–2001* (Sydney: Paper Bark Press, 2001) and *Reading the River: Selected Poems* (Highgreen, U.K.: Bloodaxe Books, 2004).

About the Author

Robert Adamson lives with his partner, photographer Juno Gemes, on the Hawkesbury River to the north of Sydney in Australia. As famous for its fierce and treacherous tides as for its prehistoric beauty, the Hawkesbury, its banks sparsely populated by humans, is home to a wide variety of avian and aquatic creatures, as well as to the land-based animals that scamper, bound, and slither through the bushlands covering its sandstone escarpments. It has been a constant presence in Adamson's life and writing. As a juvenile delinquent growing up on the shores of Sydney Harbour, he often sought refuge on the Hawkesbury at the home of his paternal grandfather, who fished its waters for over four decades. As Adamson recounts in his acclaimed autobiography *Inside Out*, his grandfather taught the future poet how to "read" the river, advising him to "never stay away too long" and imparting the instinctive knowledge that "all rivers flow into this one."

Adamson never forgot this advice, even during the dark years of reform school and personal turmoil that followed. His early reputation as a poet was that of an urban rebel and iconoclast, but he has since moved steadily beyond that; and he has always returned to the Hawkesbury River as source and refuge. In a writing career now spanning thirty-seven years, he has produced seventeen books of poetry and three books of prose. From 1970 to 1985 he was the driving force behind *New Poetry*, Australia's cutting-edge poetry magazine, and in 1987, with Juno Gemes, he established Paper Bark Press. He has won all the major Australian poetry awards and in 1994 was awarded the Fellowship of Australian Writers' Christopher Brennan Prize for a lifetime achievement in literature. *Reading the River*, a selection of his poems, was released in 2004 by the British publishing house Bloodaxe.